DAILY EXPRESS and SUNDAY EXPRESS
Cartoons
Sixtieth Series

Published By Express Newspapers, Number 10 Lower Thames Street, London EC3R 6EN

ISBN 9-780850-793192

An Introduction by

Ann Widdecombe

I have been a fan of Giles cartoons since childhood when I used to have fun spotting all the small details with their own jokes. As I grew older I began to appreciate the subtlety of the main message and now no year is complete if I haven't flipped through the Giles collection.

The cartoons are irreverent and pointed, mini satires on the society on which we live but my favourites are those with the well established characters like Grandma. There are some comedians who make you laugh even before they have said anything, their expressions alone producing peels of mirth. Grandma is their cartoon equivalent.

Giles, alas, draws no more but the cartoons are as fresh today as when they were first published. His work is a treasure trove in which people will successfully look for gems for years to come. Sardonic but not spiteful, sharp but not cruel, this is cartooning at its best.

Thank you, Giles.

ANN WIDDECOMBE

Ann Widdecombe

Family Life

GILES says: 'As usual we all made plans for Easter...

Now Turn

Daily Express, April 16, 1949

"That Scoutmaster said something when he said Scouts deserve a well earned rest after their strenuous bob-a-job week."

Sunday Express, April 13, 1958

"I didn't know I'd married an athlete until we got television."

Daily Express, June 4, 1959

"The blunt truth is that every marriage is different. The unexpected always keeps on happening ..."

Daily Express, February 5, 1963

“My wife thinks that’s ever so romantic.”

Daily Express, July 30, 1963

"Not just now, dear – there's enough trouble in the world already."

Sunday Express, January 5, 1964

"Which do you think we'll get first – 'If-cigarettes-go-up-I'm-giving-up-smoking' or 'If-beer-goes-up-I'm-giving-up-drinking'?"

Daily Express, April 14, 1964

"If anyone rescues me I'll get two weeks under the pier in the belting rain with the wife and kids."

Daily Express, August 20, 1964

"I trust I shall see something of you during the Easter Holiday?"

Daily Express, April 15, 1965

"If you haven't been phoning somebody you shouldn't, why did you fall off your chair when Miss Tapper told you she was the local telephone operator?"

Daily Express, August 24, 1965

"Anybody taking the minutes of this top-level conference?"

Daily Express, September 8, 1966

"A man can show his wife that he loves her in a thousand ways without saying it. He can show it by his look of pleasure on seeing her."

Daily Express, March 21, 1967

"You made enough noise for a dozen men when you came home from the match last night."

Sunday Express, April 16, 1967

"Mum, can our Arms to Africa debating group use the front room on Christmas Eve?"

Daily Express, December 19, 1967

"Hold it, Dad – Auntie Ivy hasn't quite gone yet."

Daily Express, December 28, 1967

"That's funny, we've been feeding them on Mummy's pills for ages."

Sunday Express, December 14, 1969

"Well somebody phoned from this address to ask us to collect a corpse."

Daily Express, April 7, 1970

"Now who's going to tell him Uncle Ernie and Auntie Rosie and the children are coming to tea?"

Sunday Express, May 31, 1970

"Mr Stevens was feeling chilly – his gas fire went out."

Daily Express, February 15, 1973

"Asking them if they've tried the Foreign Legion doesn't constitute the much-needed encouragement we are supposed to offer them, Miss Rambler."

Daily Express, March 11, 1975

"I think all this is grossly exaggerated, don't you dear?"

Daily Express, April 18, 1975

"Here we are, Einstein – a field in which you cannot fail to shine."

Daily Express, July 15, 1975

"Mine's not a Prime Minister but the thought has crossed my mind."

Sunday Express, March 13, 1977

"Never mind about Race Relationship Commissions – I'm not having Punk Pistols in my house!"

Daily Express, June 15, 1977

"I suppose your mother financed you for this Father's Day joke."

Sunday Express, June 19, 1977

"Sorry Mum, I put the clocks back instead of forward and Uncle Charlie and all of them have arrived for lunch."

Sunday Express, March 19, 1978

"Message from HQ: 'All SAS men will enter by the back door'."

Daily Express, May 8, 1980

"Some of us are not averse to violating the only on a Saturday rule."

Sunday Express, December 7, 1980

"Ahoy! Before you go – I want a word with you about my daughter!"

Sunday Express, June 28, 1981

"Pity you didn't check before you ordered a kissogram girl – the boss has brought his wife with him."

Daily Express, December 17, 1985

"You realise you are desecrating the image of one of great freedom fighters who sought to free us from the Capitalist yoke."

Sunday Express, November 2, 1986

"Don't know why Prince Andrew objects to his wife's nickname 'Fergie', I never object to everyone calling you 'Fozzie Bear'."

Daily Express, July 9, 1987

“We’ve sure got sex-equality in this house – he’s switched the washing machine on and lifted the ironing board from the cupboard all on his own.”

Daily Express, November 17, 1987

Spot the Difference

Find 10 differences between this picture and the one on the page opposite.

Answers can be found on the final page of this book

Sunday Express, February 15, 1981

CROFTS
GILES

Criminal Element

"Delegation, sir, from the clerks and others protesting about longer bank hours."

Sunday Express, October 15, 1957

"This one's the BREATHALYSER, sir – that one's the sergeant."

Sunday Express, January 24, 1960

"Yer, Honour, just because I blacked his eye and nicked him with me shiv he deliberately tweeked my ear – and I got witnesses."

Daily Express, May 19, 1964

"It's bad enough doing six months because he pinched the Chief Constable's bike without you bringing him in here laughing."

Daily Express, May 11, 1965

"I'd fancy our chances of escaping disguised as one of the guard if your outside contact had done a bit more research on uniforms."

Daily Express, November 25, 1965

"I don't fancy your chances of survival if he comes round."

Daily Express, July 6, 1967

"I must say two in the morning of November the Fifth is a strange time to be delivering barrels of frozen herrings to the House of Commons, gentlemen."

Sunday Express, November 5, 1967

"Harry – you know you worked it out they'd all be at the match guarding the ref?"

Sunday Express, November 12, 1967

"When you told me Daddy was with us in Grosvenor Square you might of mentioned Daddy was a copper."

Daily Express, October 29, 1968

"I want to phone my lawyers – he pulled my 'air."

Daily Express, August 26, 1971

"We, the local Council, consider your application to build a kennel for your Fido would constitute a violation of the rural charms of the area."

Daily Express, February 6, 1973

"Morning, Sir. How about starting the week with being in charge of an offensive weapon, parked in a No Waiting area?"

Daily Express, June 17, 1975

"Morning Judge. You know that advice you gave parents about if your boy abuses, you hit him back ..."

Daily Express, October 23, 1975

"You say it all stems from your unhappy childhood. Your Mummy wouldn't let you have a teddy bear, so at precisely one minute after kick-off you decided to boot a policeman in the face."

Daily Express, August 31, 1976

“Ernest, you did post that letter to my MP demanding the Police get a substantial wage increase immediately?”

Sunday Express, October 16, 1977

"Great for our public image – the nick bunged full of drunk and disorderly birthday revellers."

Sunday Express, September 30, 1979

"Taxi, Sir? Certainly, Sir."

Daily Express, August 20, 1981

"I wouldn't bank on M'Lud letting you off because you are unemployed – it happened to be his pad which you did up."

Sunday Express, March 18, 1984

"Hello Herbie, I didn't know you were interested in following Halley's Comet."

Daily Express, November 12, 1985

"If you exercise your right to dismiss the jury – the plaintiff confesses it was he who attacked you, and the judge is in a good mood – we might just have a chance."

Daily Express, December 3, 1985

"Frank's little joke – 'For not wearing a seat belt it is the duty of this court to send you to a place where you will be hanged by the neck until you are dead'."

Sunday Express, September 14, 1986

"You won't get off light with this one – he sentenced one of 'em yesterday to six months travel on B.R."

Daily Express, February 5, 1987

Transport

"Well, I haven't parked it IN a street with yellow bands on the lamp posts, have I?"

Daily Express, May 29, 1947

"In view of these disappearing aircraft – if anyone asks you if they can borrow a couple of destroyers, you will come and see me."

Sunday Express, September 12, 1948

"I'd like to see you drive a ____ tram up and down the ____ Embankment every ____ day of the ____ week without 'ollering for overtime."

Daily Express, December 30, 1948

"Mind you, our old car will still be running when all this new stuff is forgotten. It'll bloomin' well have to be."

Daily Express, September 29, 1949

"Next time you go on strike for seven weeks you want to make sure everybody's off the bus."

Daily Express, June 22, 1956

"What time does your ship leave, Captain?"

Daily Express, January 1, 1960

“Well, sir, if you’re seriously thinking of having her tested on Monday I shouldn’t waste your money filling her up.”

Sunday Express, September 11, 1960

"Bert's got a point there – if you're so keen on the express stopping here why can't you use your missus instead of his?"

Sunday Express, June 24, 1962

"He says he's been following the signs to Hyde Park and he's damn sure this isn't the new underground car park."

Sunday Express, October 21, 1962

"If we warn them they'll only tell us not to make a noise we'll wake Grandma."

Sunday Express, August 4, 1963

"Interesting situation, Sarge – instructor only passed his L-test yesterday and the pupil has had a provisional licence since 1935."

Daily Express, March 19, 1964

"Mum! You know you told them not to come home from the Boat Show with anything bigger than a little woolly hat?"

Daily Express, January 5, 1965

"Goodness! So we have."

Daily Express, June 24, 1965

"Dad, as a matter of interest, who tied us up?"

Daily Express, June 29, 1965

"Ho, ho, ho – someone's travel allowance gone for a burton?"

Daily Express, August 9, 1966

"Don't think I didn't see you give them a drink and say thanks very much."

Daily Express, August 1, 1967

"Faster, Bert – he's gaining on you."

Sunday Express, December 10, 1967

"Call from your sponsors, A1 – want to know why their ad is appearing upside down on TV."

Daily Express, July 16, 1968

"Let's get one of these bloody planes in the air and catch up with some sleep."

Sunday Express, April 6, 1969

"For allowing your car to be left 3 minutes beyond the allotted time on a yellow line twice in one year there is no punishment too severe. It is therefore my duty …"

Daily Express, March 19, 1970

"Would you be interested in a comfortable night in Co. Cork, Sir? We'll keep an eye on your ship."

Daily Express, April 22, 1971

"We've enjoyed waiting 40 minutes for you, Sir. I hope you enjoy the rest of the journey."

Daily Express, October 26, 1971

"I saw a very nice little cabin-cruiser at the Boat Show – sixteen-footer, just the job for me and my missus for the holidays."

Daily Express, January 5, 1976

"If you're looking for the variable-jet carburettor with constant-level fuel supply, throttle and venture, the engine is in the back."

Daily Express, January 29, 1976

"With crews like mine, no wonder they sail round the world single-handed."

Daily Express, September 5, 1977

"When I asked you where you would be putting your cross I was asking a perfectly civil question."

Sunday Express, April 15, 1979

"Penelope, I thought you told me you were a good poker player."

Daily Express, February 5, 1980

"So far she hasn't joined the chorus of witty jokes about inflation."

Sunday Express, May 18, 1980

"OK! So I had six Heads of State on board at the same time so I mista the chance!"

Daily Express, June 24, 1980

"My wife says if Mrs Thatcher can be in and out of hospital in one day and back at work the next day, so can I."

Daily Express, August 26, 1982

"We said come and spend the holiday on the boat – we didn't say anything about being afloat."

Sunday Express, May 27, 1984

"Don't ask me why – he just hit me!"

Daily Express, January 17, 1985

"Never seen the churches doing such business on a weekday. It'll be these thanksgiving services for the children going back to school."

Daily Express, September 3, 1985

"If this emergency is for another pair of oafs going treasure hunting in a six-foot plastic boat, I'm chucking 'em back!"

Daily Express, September 10, 1985

“Nice honeymoon in romantic Venice – first night in the nick!”

Daily Express, June 9, 1987

"I'll handle Horatio Nelson here, you fend off Captain Bligh."

Daily Express, January 7, 1988

Spot the Difference

Find 10 differences between this picture and the one on the page opposite.

Answers can be found on the final page of this book

Daily Express, December 24, 1982

MONOPOLY
Merry Christmas MUM
MERRY IRON
NOEL DUSTERS
DAD
Dad
Mum
25
GILES

Leisure

"This is Mr Clever-man's idea – 'Where shall we go this year to get away from it all?' we asked him. 'Tibet' he said."

Sunday Express, July 20, 1947

"How d'you like that – come in here spiv-hunting and walk off with the highest score of the week?"

Sunday Express, October 19, 1947

"Never heard Bach on the bagpipes before?"

Sunday Express, August 29, 1948

"Why – if it isn't that dear little man who wanted to see us home after the dance last night."

Daily Express, June 3, 1952

So you say there are only five types of drinker? Don't make me smile **by GILES**

Daily Express, August 13, 195

SO YOU SAY THERE ARE ONLY FIVE TYPES OF DRINKER? DON'T MAKE ME SMILE by GILES

Yo, Ho, Ho! We're not letting this one pass. According to the nonsense about the world and the bottle, this page yesterday, doctors have decided that there are five basic types of drinker. Five basic types, indeed. Without stopping to think, this hurried illustration shows at least another 19 of them, and I could go on drawing all day if it didn't mean missing opening times. Haven't the doctors met your old friend …

Number 1, the type who tells you he'd just as soon drink tea, but it's the company he likes?
Or Number 2, the type who can't drink Scotch unless it's mixed with politics?
And Number 3, the "I-work-better-when-I'm-tight" type?
And Number 4, the "Hang on, George – we might get one here in a minute" type?
And follow the numbers.
5. The knocker.
6. The "Let me tell you my sorrows."
7. The drinker who never listens to your stories, but when you've finished goes straight on with "That reminds me …"
8. Knocker.
9. "You must meet old so-and-so – he'll make you die with laughter!" An understatement, if ever.
10. "Let's have one for the road Sid."
11. Sid.
12. Knocker.
13. "If you really must know, Mr Milldew, I drink because I like it."
14. "So do I."
15. Disenchanted.
16. Two drinkers who have just treated a fellow drinker who didn't treat them back.
17. "Drink doesn't have any effect on me."
18. Watch this one. Knows lots of little tricks with matches. The drive-you-to-drink-type.
19. The abstainer.

CHEERS

"Smile, please."

Sunday Express, June 29, 1958

"This'll be a change from listening to her blaring wireless – here comes her husband."

Sunday Express, August 3, 1958

"Well, they're not down in the official entries list."

Sunday Express, August 28, 1960

"I bet Charlie's cold in goal today. By the way – where is Charlie?"

Daily Express, January 22, 1963

"That you Sergeant? I don't know if there's any connection – but Jack's treated the house the first time in 40 years."

Daily Express, August 15, 1963

"We think our Harry is fibbing when he says can he have a pint on the slate as all his private capital is invested with John Bloom."

Daily Express, July 21, 1964

"Really, Nigel, you mustn't expect everybody to want the same one elected as you do!"

Daily Express, July 27, 1965

"Why did it look suspicious? Because you went down before the fight started, that's why, Maestro."

Daily Express, October 4, 1966

"And to think we stop people coming into the country because they've got a few undesirable friends."

Daily Express, February 28, 1967

"When you've finished your lecture on what they should have done with the Torrey Canyon in the first place, I've got a little problem for you a bit nearer home."

Sunday Express, April 2, 1967

"Two iced lollies and a packet of bubbly gum ruddy well isn't what I ordered."

Sunday Express, August 13, 1967

"Harry – you're sure lucky you've got a daughter who can drive to come and fetch you."

Sunday Express, October 8, 1967

"Just one thing, fellas – you were supposed to dig this hole two hundred yards down the road."

Daily Express, June 13, 1974

'Corporal, shall we stroll over and remind them that it was on this very day someone in the Navy coined the phrase 'Kiss me, Hardy'?"

Daily Express, October 21, 1975

"Adolf Hitler in the first one, Martin Bormann in the other."

Daily Express, August 19, 1977

"Yes, dear, I did hear the stewardess say our plane is finally leaving – but you know that last hand of poker I played ...?"

Sunday Express, August 21, 1977

"Good picture of you kissing Maggie Thatcher, Lew. What yer wife think of it?"

Sunday Express, January 22, 1978

"We're in luck – Senora doesn't speak English and didn't hear our son's banal remark that her beds are a damn sight harder than the floor in London Airport."

Sunday Express, August 27, 1978

"Far enough, Adonis."

Sunday Express, August 12, 1979

"I'm not coming down to the beach with you in that!"

Sunday Express, June 15, 1980

"Hallo, Kinlay – the London office got your message that you are still stuck in a traffic jam in Zeebrugge."

Sunday Express, August 24, 1980

"Your wife's arrived with the car, Sir – to save you a tiring journey back after a hard week at the Conference."

Daily Express, September 6, 1980

"If our fishermen say they can't make a living from our waters how come the Danes are so keen to come here?"

Sunday Express, January 9, 1983

"I didn't say that our Charlie pushing the boat out means he's connected with the £7m robbery – I simply said it makes him highly suspected."

Daily Express, April 7, 1983

"We'll give them five more minutes to notice us or it will be on cardigans."

Sunday Express, August 21, 1983

"All these long sunny walks Dad's taking us on – we'll get ever so brown."

Daily Express, April 26, 1984

"Boris Becker doesn't behave like that if he loses."

Sunday Express, June 28, 1987

"Dad, remember the gentlemen you hit for playing his saxophone all the time we were delayed at Gatwick?"

Sunday Express, August 30, 1987

"Won't make a lotter difference to Harry who owns the pubs – he ain't bought a drink since they disbanded the Home Guard."

Daily Express, March 23, 1989

"She wrapped up in rugs just like the Mexicans do to keep cool. Now she wants a hot water bottle because she's too cold."

Sunday Express, August 5, 1990

Merry Christmas

"Vicar, thou hast a wolf amidst they flock."

Sunday Express, December 12, 1960

"We will maintain a more dignified performance if we refrain from continually asking Miss Jones if she had any luck."

Sunday Express, December 22, 1963

"And a Happy New Year to you – you banal, treacly mouthed patronising creep."

Daily Express, December 31, 1964

"Christmas present list please, dear."

Daily Express, November 16, 1967

"Know who I vote the Three Wise Men this Christmas? Those three who've hoofed it round the other side of the moon."

Sunday Express, December 22, 1968

Daily Express, December 24, 1973

"'George', I said, 'Christmas Eve. What better time to ask our new neighbours round for a drink and meet Mummy'."

Daily Express, December 24, 1974

"I'm having a last Bank-Holiday-of-the-fortnight party – bring Harry, Dickie, Punghi, Ronnie, Wilmer and the gang and ask Buggsie to bring his drums and Hi-fi with him."

Sunday Express, January 2, 1977

"You can get that damn thing off my desk for a start!"

Daily Express, December 19, 1977

"We Three Kings of Orient are ..."

Sunday Express, December 23, 1984

"Good news – the builders who started on your storm damage repairs asked me to tell you they'll be back early in the New Year."

Sunday Express, December 13, 1987

"You must expect a few pellets in your backside, Vicar – cutting through here delivering free pheasants to the needy."

Sunday Express, December 20, 1987

Spot the Difference

Find 10 differences between this picture and the one on the page opposite.

Answers can be found on the final page of this book

Daily Express, December 24, 1981

RACING SPECIAL
GILES

Spot the Difference Answers

February 15, 1981

December 24, 1982

December 24, 1981

The publisher wishes to thank Derek Unsworth for his help and assistance in compiling the 2007 collection.

Editor's Note:

Due to the fact some of these cartoons are taken from our newspaper archive, there may be a variation in the reproduction.

Reproduced by Wyndeham-Icon. Produced by Polskabook. Printed and bound in Poland EU.